Dream Big!
Sonja Biggs
BRANDON

Brandon's Dream
By Sonja Biggs
Photos by Atom Biggs

Once upon a time there was an ordinary little boy who had a very big dream.

He was just like every other little boy. He played and laughed with his little brother.

He made cookies with his friends and then ate them all up, too!

Brandon loved holidays and hunting for Easter eggs with the neighbors.

Sometimes he and his brother had soap bubble fights in the living room.

Brandon ran track and cross country. He ran fast and did his very best.

Brandon loved playing games at birthday parties...even worm birthday parties!

He raised lambs for 4-H and won Grand Champion overall.

He also won Grand Champion for his dramatic speeches.

Just like other kids, Brandon loved to make yummy creations in the kitchen.

He enjoyed dressing up to go to Rennaisance Faires, too.

Being a clown helped bring Brandon a little closer to his dream.

He made the lives of many children a little brighter and happier.

Brandon enjoyed riding bikes with his friends, just like most kids do.

He even took a princess to her prom.

Halloween parties were the best. Brandon could dress up to be his favorite theater characters like the Phantom from The Phantom of the Opera.

It was difficult to remember that Brandon could not see...not like some of you and me...Brandon was blind.

Brandon's greatest dream was to become an actor and singer performing on the stage.

So he practiced.

And practiced.

He learned to move and dance.

He learned to act and sing.

Then one day Brandon took his talents to the stage.

He even performed on film.

He loved his role as Rolf in Sound of Music.

He had fun being a knight in Camelot.

He even sang and danced his way to Belle as the Prince in Beauty and the Beast.

These are magical moments for one ordinary boy who sees only through touch, hearing, smell, and taste; but most of all who sees with his heart.

Brandon's dreams are still coming true.

Brandon wants you to follow your dreams...whether you can see with your eyes or not... follow the vision that lives in your heart and your dreams can come true, too.

Dream the impossible dream...then live it!